Easy & Irresistible
Word Family Poems & Puppets

20 Reproducible Poems & Make-and-Take Paperbag Puppets That Teach Key Word Families and Build Phonics Skills

SCHOLASTIC
PROFESSIONAL BOOKS

New York • Toronto • London • Auckland • Sydney
Mexico City • New Delhi • Hong Kong • Buenos Aires

ACKNOWLEDGMENTS

"Gabby Crab," "Blue Jay," "Panda Pam," "Ben's Hen," "Banana Split,"
and "Little Bug" by Helen O'Reilly.

"That Cat!" by Jaime Lucero.

"The Tiny Squid," "Bear on a Swing," "The Snow Family,"
"Butterfly on My Book," and "Clean Cub Club"
copyright © by Kathleen Hollenbeck.

Cover and interior design by John Furlong

Interior illustrations by Maxie Chambliss

ISBN 0-439-25183-4

Copyright © 2002 Deborah V. Hillstead and Marjorie V. Fields

Printed in the U.S.A.

1 2 3 4 5 6 7 8 9 10   40   08 07 06 05 04 03 02

TABLE OF CONTENTS

Poems & Puppets with "a" sounds

Poems & Puppets with "e" sounds

Poems & Puppets with "i" sounds

Poems & Puppets with "o" sounds

Poems & Puppets with "u" sounds

Introduction

Welcome to *Easy & Irresistible Word Family Poems & Puppets*. These lively and highly entertaining poems and puppets build children's early reading and writing skills and teach phonics in a meaningful way. Each of the 20 poems in this book features a different word family (also called a rime, phonogram, or word chunk).

Rhyming words in a poem help children develop phonemic awareness as they listen for similarities and differences in the sounds the words make. Rhymes with the same spelling (those that belong to the same word family) boost children's literacy skills even more. Children will discover that for each word family that they learn, they can read and spell many new words. For instance, learning the *-ot* word family will help them read and write *dot, cot, pot, tot, lot, not, got,* and *rot,* as well as *shot, blot, trot,* and so on.

In fact, the 38 most common phonograms can make 654 one-syllable words when combined with different beginning consonants. (Note: Watch out for words that sound the same but are not spelled the same. For example, *honey* and *funny, great* and *eight,* and *hi* and *bye.* These are fine to play around with orally when teaching phonemic awareness, but do not use them to help beginners read with phonics.)

Teaching With the Poems

Select a poem and copy it onto chart paper or sentence strip paper, making sure the print is large and clear. Gather your students together and read through the poem, helping them enjoy the silliness or fun of the content. This will help children focus on getting meaning and enjoyment from reading.

Read the poem again, pointing to each word as you say it, and invite children to read along with you. Repeat the reading with the children, helping them to hear the rhymes and to see how they are written. Using an attractive pointer (see page 6) helps focus children's attention on the print. Repeat this shared reading activity as often as children enjoy it.

When children see what specific words look like in print, they get vital information on how reading and writing "work." Your students will want to explore this information further on their own, so it is important to have the poem charts and the pointers

Organizing and Storing the Poems

How can you make your poems and story charts readily available to students so they can practice reading with them? Try skirt hangers—the ones with clips, of course! You can put over-the-door hooks on your doors on which to hang the poems, or attach coat hooks to cabinets or walls. Hooks on walls around the classroom give children many places to hang the charts and read from them.

To store the poems and charts, buy inexpensive unassembled closet racks. Once assembled, these racks offer easy storage—especially when your charts are already on skirt hangers!

available as a choice-time activity. To further emphasize the rimes, you may want to encourage children to match a variety of word beginnings (called the "onset") with a given ending (the rime).

Making a Pointer

Use this pointer to direct children's attention to specific words and letters during shared reading of the poems.

You need:

- One child- or adult-sized garden glove
- Polyester fiberfill stuffing (from a craft or fabric store)
- 18-inch-long dowel, about $\frac{1}{4}$-inch in diameter
- Needle and thread
- Wooden bead to fit the end of the dowel (from a craft store)
- Hot-glue gun and glue sticks
- $\frac{1}{2}$-yard colored ribbon

Directions:

1. Loosely stuff the glove with polyester fiberfill.

2. Insert the dowel into the glove, positioning it so that it goes to the end of the "pointer" finger.

3. Thread a needle and knot the end. Make running stitches around the cuff of the glove to hold the dowel in place. Pull the thread tight and tie it off.

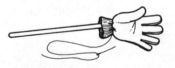

4. Use the hot-glue gun to glue the inside wrist of the glove to the dowel.

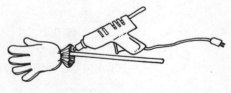

5. Glue down the other three fingers and the thumb of the glove to make a pointing hand. You can sew the fingers instead if you prefer.

6. Tie a bow at the wrist using the colored ribbon.

7. Glue the wooden bead to the other end of the dowel.

Using Puppets to Strengthen the Home-School Connection

Experienced teachers know how important it is to keep parents informed and involved. When parents understand what you are doing at school, they tend to be more helpful and supportive. As a result, their children do better in school.

This is why we've included easy step-by-step directions for making puppets to accompany the poems. Children will enjoy making these adorable puppets that feature the main characters in the word-family poems.

After children have finished assembling each puppet, give them a copy of the matching poem to glue to the back of their puppet. Then encourage them to take home the puppets with the poems and share them with their families. We've found that families are much more likely to read the poems together when they're on a puppet rather than on a plain sheet of paper.

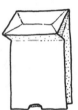

Puppet-Making Basics

Each poem in this book features a different puppet and easy-to-follow directions for how to make it. However, there are some basic features that are common to most of the puppets.

First, all of the puppets start out with small paper lunch bags. All but the squid use a 6-inch circle for the head and a 6- by 9-inch rectangle for the body. They also use a 3- by 6-inch rectangle as the basis for the mouth piece, which is built into the bag's bottom flap.

You don't need to use a ruler to measure most of the pieces because they are easy-to-identify segments of the 9- by 12-inch construction paper you already have in your classroom. For instance, the body piece (a 6- by 9-inch rectangle) is half of the sheet. All you have to do is fold a sheet of construction paper in half and cut on the fold.

The 6- by 6-inch head piece can be cut from the remaining half, leaving a 3- by 6-inch piece that is easily segmented into the $1\frac{1}{2}$-inch squares for eyes and ears. You may want to ask parent volunteers to help you cut out the pieces.

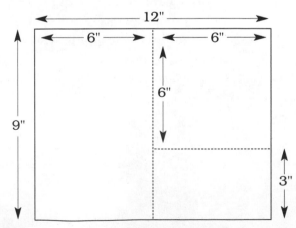

Teaching Children How to Cut Without Tracing

To encourage children's thinking skills, we provide them with squares for the head and eyes, then show them how to cut around the corners to "find the circle hiding in the square." This helps them discover the relationship between the two shapes.

To show children how to cut off just the corners of the square, tell them to point their scissors to the ceiling and turn the paper. Ask them, "Am I cutting off big pieces of the corners or little ones?" *(Little ones)* Show them that they will have four small scraps of paper when they are done.

This same process works for making a rectangle with one rounded edge. Tell the children to cut or round off two corners on one short side to make ears, arms, or tail. To make the mouth pieces, children will have to round off two corners on one long side. Make sure children know about the pieces that they're making, not just about cutting. Knowing what they are making will help them think about where to cut.

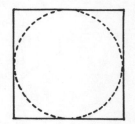

Kindergartners love the "magic" of cutting two pieces at once! This certainly helps to make both eyes, both ears, and both arms the same size. Tell your students, "Cut two pieces together because it's quicker and they'll look the same." You can show them how to hold two little squares and cut two eyes or ears at once, or how to hold two rectangles and make both arms at once.

Can Kindergartners Do It?

Can kindergartners really make these puppets and do it without tracing anything? Yes, they can. They can because they are taught to think about what they are doing. Of course, they don't start with the most intricate puppets at the beginning of the year. In fact, a good first lesson about "finding the circle hiding in the square" can be cutting out red circles to make apples for name tags. As the year progresses, you can introduce progressively more complex tasks.

Basic Directions for Assembling the Puppets

Complete step-by-step directions for how to make the puppets appear on the teacher pages after each poem. However, here are some basic directions to start with:

1. To glue the circle for the head to the paper lunch bag, put four drops of glue on the bag's bottom flap (not on the circle). Demonstrate to children how to put a drop (not a puddle) of glue on each corner of the flap. Then position the head so that all the corners of the flap are covered.

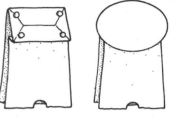

2. To attach the body, lift the bag's flap and put four drops of glue like buttons down the center of the bag. Attach the 6- by 9-inch rectangle so that the top is positioned right below the flap's fold. Notice that only the middle of the paper is glued to the paper bag, leaving the sides open for attaching arms, legs, or wings.

3. After cutting out the mouth piece, lift the bag's flap again and glue it right below the fold. The mouth will cover the top of the body, but that's fine.

4. To attach the legs (or arms or wings), glue them between the rectangular body piece and the paper bag.

5. Directions for the rest of the puppet will differ depending on the puppet itself.

Tips for Gluing

To make the glue stick, tell children to "hold it and hold it until it gets warm." Extra glue oozing out? Use scrap paper to scrape it off.

Gabby Crab

Hello, my name is Abby.
I'm just a little crab.
My brother says I'm blabby
Because I love to gab.
I gab when days are sunny.
I gab with my friend Bab.
I gab in elevators
And in a taxicab.

TAXI

CRAB CAB
COMPANY

-ab Word Family

Ask children to look for words in the poem that contain the letters -ab. List them on chart paper. Encourage children to think of other words that belong in the -ab word family. Add their words to the list.

Word List

crab   gab   Bab   taxicab

Making a Crab Puppet

This crab puppet is the perfect companion to "Gabby Crab." Help children glue a copy of the poem to the back of the puppet. Encourage them to take it home to share with their families.

Each child needs:

• one small paper bag
• 6- by 6-inch red square (head)
• 6- by 9-inch red rectangle (body)
• two 4 ½- by 2-inch red rectangles (arms)
• two 2- by 2-inch red squares (claws)
• eight 4 ½- by 1-inch red rectangles (legs)
• two 1- by 3-inch yellow rectangles (eye stalks)
• two 1- by 1-inch black squares (eyeballs)
• 3- by 6-inch yellow rectangle (mouth)
• scissors
• glue
• black crayon or marker

Directions (Review "Puppet-Making Basics," pages 7–9.)

1. To make the head and body:

•   Use the scissors to round off all the corners of the 6-inch red square to make a circle.
•   Glue the head onto the paper bag's flap (bottom).
•   Lift the head and fold back the flap. Put four drops of glue down the center of the bag.
•   Press the 6- by 9-inch red rectangle to the bag under the flap.

2. To make the arms:

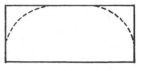

- Hold both 4½- by 2-inch red rectangles together. Use the scissors to round off the two corners on one long side and create a curved side, as shown.

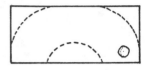

- Holding the curved sides, cut an arch on the other long side to create a C shape.

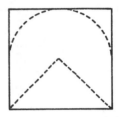

- Put a dot of glue on the front and back of one end of each arm piece.
- Glue the arms between the bag and body just below the crab's head and press.

3. To make the claws:

- Hold both 2-inch red squares together. Round off two corners of the squares.
- Hold the pieces with the square end down and scissors pointing to the ceiling. Cut a V shape into the square end, as shown.
- Put a dot of glue on the end of each arm. Press the rounded side of the claw on the glue.

4. To make the legs:

- Fold all eight 4½- by 1-inch red rectangles accordion-style.
- Put a dot of glue on the front and back of one end of each leg.
- Glue four legs on each side of the puppet between the bag and body. Start below the arms and work your way down.

5. To make the eyes:

- Fold both 1- by 3-inch yellow rectangles accordion-style.
- Put a drop of glue on one end of each folded eyestalk. Glue them to the middle of the crab's face.
- Hold both small black squares together. Use the scissors to round off the corners to make circles.
- Put a drop of glue on each black circle. Glue a circle to the end of each eyestalk.

6. To make the mouth:

- Use the scissors to round off two corners on one long side of the 3- by 6-inch yellow rectangle to make a half circle.
- Lift the flap and put four drops of glue just below the flap fold. Glue the straight side of the mouth against the fold.
- Use a black crayon or marker to draw a smile along the bottom edge of the head.
- Holding the puppet's mouth open, use the crayon or marker to outline the edge of the lower mouth.

That Cat!

That big fat cat
Sat on Aunt Pat's hat,
And now it's flat
As a welcome mat.
Now when Aunt Pat
Comes to sit and chat
She wears on her head
A big flat hat.

-at Word Family

Ask children to look for words in the poem that contain the letters -at. List them on chart paper. Encourage children to think of other words that belong in the -at word family. Add their words to the list.

Word List

that	cat	fat	sat	Pat
hat	flat	mat	chat	

Making a Cat Puppet

Children will love making this cat puppet to go with the poem "That Cat!" Help them glue a copy of the poem to the back of the puppet. Encourage them to take it home to share with their families.

Each child needs:

- one small paper bag
- 6- by 6-inch black square (head)
- 6- by 9-inch black rectangle (body)
- two 4½- by 2-inch black rectangles (arms)
- two 1½- by 1½-inch yellow squares (eyeballs)
- two 1- by 1-inch blue squares (eyes)
- 3- by 6-inch red rectangle (mouth)
- 1- by 1-inch red square (nose)
- 2- by 2-inch black square (ears)
- scissors
- glue
- white or pink crayon or marker

Directions (Review "Puppet-Making Basics," pages 7–9.)

1. To make the head and body:

- Use the scissors to round off all the corners of the 6-inch black square to make a circle.
- Glue the head onto the paper bag's flap (bottom).
- Lift the head and fold back the flap. Put four drops of glue down the center of the paper bag.
- Press the 6- by 9-inch black rectangle to the bag under the flap.

2. To make the arms:

- Hold both 4½- by 2-inch black rectangles together. Use the scissors to round off two corners on one short side.
- Put a dot of glue on the front and back of the squared end of each arm piece.
- Glue the arms between the bag and body just below the cat's head and press.

3. To make the eyes:

- Hold both yellow squares together. Use the scissors to round off all the corners to make circles.
- Repeat with the blue squares.
- Put a drop of glue on each yellow circle. Press the yellow eyeballs near the middle of the head.
- Put a drop of glue on each blue circle and press one to the center of each yellow eyeball.

4. To make the mouth:

- Use the scissors to round off the two corners on one long side of the red rectangle to make a half circle.
- Lift the flap and put four drops of glue just below the flap fold. Glue the straight side of the mouth against the fold.
- Use a white or pink crayon or marker to draw a smile on the cat's face.
- Holding the puppet's mouth open, use the crayon or marker to outline the edge of the lower mouth.

5. To make the nose:

- Use the scissors to round off all the corners of the red square to make a circle. (Or, you can cut out a triangular nose.)
- Put a drop of glue on the nose and place it on the cat's face about halfway between the eyes and upper lip.

6. To make the ears:

- Cut the 2-inch black square diagonally in half.
- Put two drops of glue on one side of each triangle. Glue the ears on the back of the head near the top.

16

Blue Jay

Blue jay, blue jay,
Please stay and play.
Don't fly away,
Stay here
All day.
We can play
With blocks or clay
If you will stay
With me all day.

-ay Word Family

Ask children to look for words in the poem that contain the letters -ay. List them on chart paper. Encourage children to think of other words that belong in the -ay word family. Add their words to the list.

Word List

jay	stay	play
away	day	clay

Making a Blue Jay Puppet

Invite children to make this blue jay puppet for the poem "Blue Jay." Then help them glue a copy of the poem to the back of the puppet. Encourage them to take it home to share with their families.

Each child needs:

- one small paper bag
- 6- by 6-inch blue square (head)
- 6- by 9-inch blue rectangle (body)
- two 4- by 4-inch blue squares (wings)
- two 1½- by 1½-inch white squares (eyeballs)
- two 1- by 1-inch blue squares (eyes)
- 3- by 6-inch yellow rectangle (mouth)
- 4- by 4-inch yellow square (beak)
- scissors
- glue

Directions (Review "Puppet-Making Basics," pages 7–9.)

1. To make the head and body:
- Use the scissors to round off all the corners of the 6-inch blue square to make a circle.
- Glue the head onto the paper bag's flap (bottom).
- Lift the head and fold back the flap. Put four drops of glue down the center of the paper bag.
- Press the blue rectangle to the bag under the flap.

2. To make the wings:
- Hold the two 4-inch blue squares together. Use the scissors to round off one corner, as shown.
- Put three dots of glue on the front and back of the squared end of each wing.
- Glue the wings between the bag and body just below the bird's head and press.

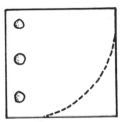

3. To make the eyes:
- Hold both white squares together. Use the scissors to round off all the corners to make circles.
- Repeat with the 1-inch blue squares.
- Put a drop of glue on each white circle. Press the white eyeballs near the middle of the head.
- Put a drop of glue on each blue circle and place one at the center of each white eyeball.

4. To make the mouth:
- Use the scissors to round off two corners on one long side of the yellow rectangle to make a half circle.
- Lift the flap and put four drops of glue just below the flap fold. Glue the straight side of the mouth against the fold.

5. To make the beak:
- Cut the yellow square diagonally in half.
- Put three drops of glue on the longest side of each triangle, as shown.
- Glue one triangle to the blue jay's upper lip and the other triangle under the curved edge of the mouth. Be careful not to glue the mouth shut!

Panda Pam

I'm a panda,
Yes I am!
I'm proud to say
My name is Pam.
I like to eat
Some honey ham,
And for dessert,
A little jam.

JAM

-am Word Family

Ask children to look for words in the poem that contain the letters -am. List them on chart paper. Encourage children to think of other words that belong in the -am word family. Add their words to the list.

Word List

Pam   am   ham   jam

Making a Panda Puppet

Who can resist this adorable panda puppet that goes with "Panda Pam"? Help children glue a copy of the poem to the back of the puppet. Encourage them to take it home to share with their families.

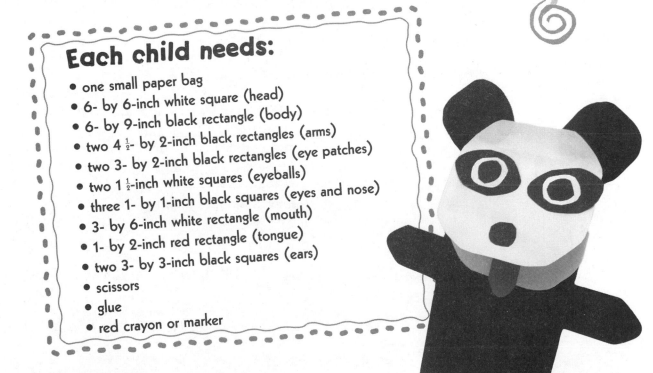

Each child needs:
- one small paper bag
- 6- by 6-inch white square (head)
- 6- by 9-inch black rectangle (body)
- two 4 $\frac{1}{2}$- by 2-inch black rectangles (arms)
- two 3- by 2-inch black rectangles (eye patches)
- two 1 $\frac{1}{2}$-inch white squares (eyeballs)
- three 1- by 1-inch black squares (eyes and nose)
- 3- by 6-inch white rectangle (mouth)
- 1- by 2-inch red rectangle (tongue)
- two 3- by 3-inch black squares (ears)
- scissors
- glue
- red crayon or marker

Directions (Review "Puppet-Making Basics," pages 7–9.)

1. To make the head and body:
- Use the scissors to round off all the corners of the 6-inch white square to make a circle.
- Glue the head onto the paper bag's flap (bottom).
- Lift the head and fold back the flap. Put four drops of glue down the center of the paper bag.
- Press the 6- by 9-inch black rectangle to the bag under the flap.

2. To make the arms:

- Hold both 4$\frac{1}{2}$- by 2-inch black rectangles together. Use the scissors to round off two corners on one short side.
- Put a drop of glue on the front and back of the squared end of each arm piece.
- Glue the arms between the bag and body just below the panda's head and press.

3. To make the eyes:

- Hold both 3- by 2-inch black rectangles together. Use the scissors to round off all the corners to make ovals.
- Hold both 1$\frac{1}{2}$-inch white squares together. Use the scissors to round off all the corners to make circles.
- Repeat with two 1-inch black squares.
- Put a drop of glue on each black oval. Press both ovals near the middle of the head.
- Put a drop of glue on each white circle and place one at the center of each black oval.
- Put a drop of glue on each black circle and press one to the center of each white eyeball.

4. To make the mouth:

- Use the scissors to round off two corners on one long side of the 3- by 6-inch white rectangle to make a half circle.
- Lift the flap and put four drops of glue just below the flap fold. Glue the straight side of the mouth against the fold.
- Use a red crayon or marker to draw a smile along the bottom edge of the head.
- Holding the puppet's mouth open, use the crayon or marker to outline the edge of the lower mouth.

5. To make the tongue:

- Use the scissors to round off two corners on one short side of the red rectangle.
- Put a drop of glue on the short straight side of the tongue. Glue the tongue to the center of the mouth.

6. To make the nose:

- Use the scissors to round off all the corners of the remaining 1-inch black square to make a circle.
- Put a drop of glue on the black nose and place it about halfway between the eyes and upper lip.

7. To make the ears:

- Hold both 3-inch black squares together. Use the scissors to round off all the corners to make circles.
- Glue the ears on the back of the head near the top.

The Little Bee

A little yellow bee
Buzzed around a tree.
"Look at what I made,
Come and see!
Peek into my hive,
Sweets are yours for free!"

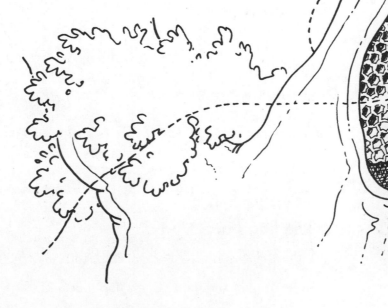

-ee Word Family

Ask children to look for words in the poem that contain the letters -ee. List them on chart paper. Encourage children to think of other words that belong in the -ee word family. Add their words to the list.

Word List

bee   tree   see   free

Making a Bee Puppet

This bee puppet is sure to delight children who enjoyed the poem "The Little Bee." Help children glue a copy of the poem to the back of the puppet. Encourage them to take it home to share with their families.

Each child needs:

- one small paper bag
- 6- by 6-inch yellow square (head)
- 6- by 9-inch yellow rectangle (body)
- two 4- by 4-inch black squares (wings)
- eight 4½- by 1-inch black rectangles (legs and antennae)
- four 1- by 6-inch black rectangles (stripes)
- two 1½- by 1½-inch black squares (eyeballs)
- two 1-inch yellow squares (eyes)
- 3- by 6-inch black rectangle (mouth)
- scissors
- glue
- black crayon or marker

Directions (Review "Puppet-Making Basics," pages 7–9.)

1. To make the head and body:

- Use the scissors to round off all the corners of the 6-inch yellow square to make a circle.
- Glue the head onto the paper bag's flap (bottom).

- Lift the head and fold back the flap. Put four drops of glue down the center of the paper bag.
- Press the yellow rectangle to the bag under the flap.

2. To make the wings:

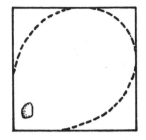

- Hold both 4-inch black squares together. Use the scissors to round off three corners of the squares, as shown.
- Put a drop of glue on the front and back of the remaining corner of each wing.
- Glue the wings between the bag and body just below the bee's head and press.

3. To make the legs:

- Fold six $4\frac{1}{2}$- by 1-inch black rectangles accordion-style. Put a dot of glue on the front and back of one end of each leg piece.
- Glue three legs on each side of the bee, between the bag and body. Start just below the wings and work down.

4. To make the stripes:

- Put three drops of glue on each 1- by 6-inch black rectangle.
- Glue the stripes on the body to make a pattern (black, yellow, black, yellow, black, and so on).

5. To make the eyes:

- Hold both $1\frac{1}{2}$-inch black squares together. Use the scissors to round off all the corners to make circles.
- Repeat with the 1-inch yellow squares.
- Put a drop of glue on each black circle. Press the black eyeballs near the middle of the head.
- Put a drop of glue on each yellow circle and place one at the center of each black eyeball.

6. To make the mouth:

- Use the scissors to round off two corners on one long side of the 3- by 6-inch black rectangle to make a half circle.
- Lift the flap and put four drops of glue just below the flap fold. Glue the straight side of the mouth against the fold.
- Use a black crayon or marker to draw a smile along the bottom edge of the head.

7. To make the antennae:

- Put a drop of glue on one end of the remaining two $4\frac{1}{2}$- by 1-inch black rectangles.
- Glue the antennae on the back of the head near the top.

Ben's Hen

I have a friend.
His name is Ben.
And in his yard
He has a pen.
And in that pen
He has a hen.
I visit him
Now and then.

-en Word Family

Ask children to look for words in the poem that contain the letters -en. List them on chart paper. Encourage children to think of other words that belong in the -en word family. Add their words to the list.

Word List

Ben   hen   pen   then

Making a Hen Puppet

This hen puppet makes a wonderful companion to the poem "Ben's Hen." Help children glue a copy of the poem to the back of the puppet. Encourage them to take it home to share with their families.

Each child needs:

- one small paper bag
- 6- by 6-inch red square (head)
- 6- by 9-inch red rectangle (body)
- two 4- by 4-inch red squares (wings)
- two 1½- by 1½-inch white squares (eyes)
- two 1- by 1-inch blue squares (eyeballs)
- 3- by 6-inch yellow rectangle (mouth)
- 4- by 4-inch yellow square (beak)
- 3- by 3-inch orange square (comb)
- 4- by 4-inch red square (tail, optional)
- scissors
- glue

Directions (Review "Puppet-Making Basics," pages 7–9.)

1. To make the head and body:

- Use the scissors to round off all the corners of the 6-inch red square to make a circle.
- Glue the head onto the paper bag's flap (bottom).
- Lift the head and fold back the flap. Put four drops of glue down the center of the paper bag.
- Press the red rectangle to the bag under the flap.

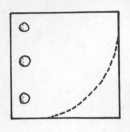

2. To make the wings:

- Hold the two 4-inch red squares together. Use the scissors to round off one corner, as shown.
- Put three dots of glue on the front and back of the squared end of each wing.
- Glue the wings between bag and body just below the hen's head and press.

3. To make the eyes:

- Hold both white squares together. Use the scissors to round off all the corners to make circles.
- Repeat with the blue squares.
- Put a drop of glue on each white circle. Press the white eyeballs near the middle of the head.
- Put a drop of glue on each blue circle and place one at the center of each white eyeball.

4. To make the mouth:

- Use the scissors to round off two corners on one long side of the yellow rectangle to make a half circle.
- Lift the flap and put four drops of glue just below the flap fold. Glue the straight side of the mouth against the fold.

5. To make the beak:

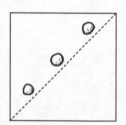

- Cut the yellow square diagonally in half.
- Put three drops of glue on the longest side of each triangle, as shown.
- Glue one triangle to the hen's upper lip and the other triangle under the curved edge of the mouth. Be careful not to glue the mouth shut!

6. To make the comb:

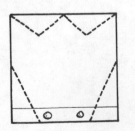

- Cut off two corners of one side of the orange square.
- Cut two V-shaped pieces from the opposite side, as shown.
- Fold the narrow end over about one inch. Put two drops of glue on the folded end and glue the comb to the top of the hen's head.

7. To make the tail (optional):

- Using a 4-inch red square, repeat the steps in #6 above to make the tail.
- Glue the tail to the back of the hen puppet, leaving enough room for the poem.

Red Ant's Sled

A red ant named Ted
Had a shiny new sled.
Down, down the hill he sped
And ran into a shed.
Crash!
    Bang!
        Boom!
            Ouch!
Poor Ted went to bed.

-ed Word Family

Ask children to look for words in the poem that contain the letters -ed. List them on chart paper. Encourage children to think of other words that belong in the -ed word family. Add their words to the list.

Word List

red	Ted	sled
sped	shed	bed

Making an Ant Puppet

Children will enjoy making this playful ant puppet to go with the poem "Red Ant's Sled." Help them glue a copy of the poem to the back of the puppet. Encourage them to take it home to share with their families.

Each child needs:

- one small paper bag
- 6- by 6-inch red square (head)
- 6- by 9-inch red rectangle (body)
- six 4 ½- by 1-inch red rectangles (legs)
- four 1 ½- by 1 ½-inch yellow squares (eyeballs and hands)
- two 1- by 1-inch black squares (eyes)
- 3- by 6-inch yellow rectangle (mouth)
- two 4 ½- by ½-inch black rectangles (antennae)
- scissors
- glue
- black crayon or marker

Directions (Review "Puppet-Making Basics," pages 7–9.)

1. To make the head and body:

- Use the scissors to round off all the corners of the red square to make a circle.
- Glue the head onto the paper bag's flap (bottom).
- Lift the head and fold back the flap. Put four drops of glue down the center of the paper bag.
- Press the 6- by 9-inch red rectangle to the bag under the flap.

2. To make the legs:

- Fold the 4½- by 1-inch red rectangles accordion-style. Put a dot of glue on the front and back of one end of each leg.
- Glue three legs on each side of the ant, between the bag and body. Start just below the head and work down.

3. To make the eyes:

- Hold two yellow squares together. Use the scissors to round off all the corners to make circles.
- Repeat with the black squares.
- Put a drop of glue on each yellow circle. Press the yellow eyeballs near the middle of the head.
- Put a drop of glue on each black circle and place one at the center of each yellow eyeball.

4. To make the mouth:

- Use the scissors to round off two corners on one long side of the yellow rectangle to make a half circle.
- Lift the flap and put four drops of glue just below the flap fold. Glue the straight side of the mouth against the fold.
- Use a black crayon or marker to draw a smile along the bottom edge of the head.
- Holding the puppet's mouth open, use the crayon or marker to outline the edge of the lower mouth.

5. To make the nose:

- Draw two dots with the black crayon or marker in the center of the ant's face near its upper lip.

6. To make the antennae:

- Put a drop of glue on one short end of each black rectangle.
- Glue the antennae on the back of the head near the top.

7. To make the hands:

- Hold the two remaining yellow squares together. Use the scissors to round off all the corners to make circles.
- Glue the yellow hands to the ends of the top two legs.

Sheep's Noisy Jeep

A playful sheep
Drove in a jeep
Up a hill that was steep.
He honked the horn,
Beep! Beep! Beep!
None of us could sleep!
We said to him:
"Stop that beep,
Or no more jeep!"

-eep Word Family

Ask children to look for words in the poem that contain the letters -eep. List them on chart paper. Encourage children to think of other words that belong in the -eep word family. Add their words to the list.

Word List

sheep   jeep   steep   beep   sleep

Making a Sheep Puppet

This adorable sheep puppet is a great prop to use with the poem "Sheep's Noisy Jeep." Help children glue a copy of the poem to the back of the puppet. Encourage them to take it home to share with their families.

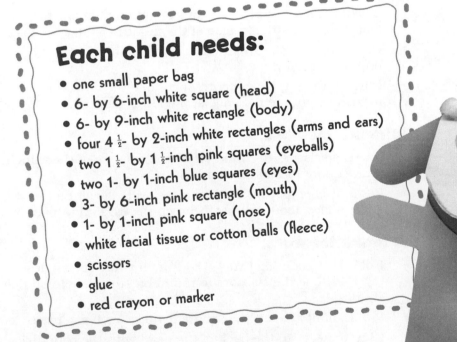

Each child needs:

- one small paper bag
- 6- by 6-inch white square (head)
- 6- by 9-inch white rectangle (body)
- four 4 ½- by 2-inch white rectangles (arms and ears)
- two 1 ½- by 1 ½-inch pink squares (eyeballs)
- two 1- by 1-inch blue squares (eyes)
- 3- by 6-inch pink rectangle (mouth)
- 1- by 1-inch pink square (nose)
- white facial tissue or cotton balls (fleece)
- scissors
- glue
- red crayon or marker

Directions (Review "Puppet-Making Basics," pages 7–9.)

1. To make the head and body:

- Use the scissors to round off all the corners of the white square to make a circle.
- Glue the head onto the paper bag's flap (bottom).
- Lift the head and fold back the flap. Put four drops of glue down the center of the paper bag.
- Press the 6- by 9-inch white rectangle to the bag under the flap.

2. To make the arms:

- Hold two $4\frac{1}{2}$- by 2-inch white rectangles together. Use the scissors to round off two corners on one short side.
- Put a dot of glue on the front and back of the squared end of each arm piece.
- Glue the arms between the bag and body just below the sheep's head and press.

3. To make the eyes:

- Hold both $1\frac{1}{2}$-inch pink squares together. Use the scissors to round off all the corners to make circles.
- Repeat with the blue squares.
- Put a drop of glue on each pink circle. Press the pink eyeballs near the middle of the head.
- Put a drop of glue on each blue circle and place one at the center of each pink eyeball.

4. To make the mouth:

- Use the scissors to round off two corners on one long side of the pink rectangle to make a half circle.
- Lift the flap and put four drops of glue just below the flap fold. Glue the straight side of the mouth against the fold.
- Use a red crayon or marker to draw a smile along the bottom edge of the head.
- Holding the puppet's mouth open, use the crayon or marker to outline the edge of the lower mouth.

5. To make the nose:

- Use the scissors to round off all the corners of the 1-inch pink square to make a circle.
- Put a drop of glue on the pink nose and place it on the sheep's face about halfway between the eyes and upper lip.

6. To make the ears:

- Hold the remaining two $4\frac{1}{2}$- by 2-inch white rectangles together. Use the scissors to round off two corners on one short side.
- Put a dot of glue on the squared end of each ear piece.
- Glue the ears to the back of the head with the rounded ends pointing downward.

7. To make the fleece:

- Put several drops of glue on top of the sheep's head between its ears.
- Tear tissue into small pieces or use cotton balls and press the fleece lightly into the glue.

Dancing Pig

Here comes the pig
Wearing a wig.
She likes to dance
And do a jig.

Here comes the pig.
Isn't she big?
We love to watch
Her dance the jig.

-ig Word Family

Ask children to look for words in the poem that contain the letters -ig. List them on chart paper. Encourage children to think of other words that belong in the -ig word family. Add their words to the list.

Word List

pig   wig   jig   big

Making a Pig Puppet

Bring the lovable "Dancing Pig" to life with this easy-to-make pig puppet. Help children glue a copy of the poem to the back of the puppet. Encourage them to take it home to share with their families.

Each child needs:

- one small paper bag
- 6- by 6-inch purple square (head)
- 6- by 9-inch purple rectangle (body)
- two 4 $\frac{1}{2}$- by 2-inch purple rectangles (arms)
- two 1 $\frac{1}{2}$- by 1 $\frac{1}{2}$-inch white squares (eyeballs)
- two 1- by 1-inch blue squares (eyes)
- 3- by 6-inch light-pink rectangle (mouth)
- 2- by 2-inch light-pink square (nose)
- 1- by 2-inch red rectangle (tongue)
- 3- by 3-inch purple square (ears)
- scissors
- glue
- red crayon or marker

Directions (Review "Puppet-Making Basics," pages 7–9.)

1. To make the head and body:

- Use the scissors to round off all the corners of the 6-inch purple square to make a circle.
- Glue the head onto the paper bag's flap (bottom).
- Lift the head and fold back the flap. Put four drops of glue down the center of the paper bag.
- Press the 6- by 9-inch purple rectangle to the bag under the flap.

2. To make the arms:

- Hold both 4$\frac{1}{2}$- by 2-inch purple rectangles together. Use the scissors to round off two corners on one short side.
- Put a dot of glue on the front and back of the squared end of each arm piece.
- Glue the arms between the bag and body just below the pig's head and press.

3. To make the eyes:

- Hold both white squares together. Use the scissors to round off all the corners to make circles.
- Repeat with the blue squares.
- Put a drop of glue on each white circle. Press the white eyeballs near the middle of the head.
- Put a drop of glue on each blue circle and place one at the center of each white eyeball.

4. To make the mouth:

- Use the scissors to round off two corners on one long side of the light-pink rectangle to make a half circle.
- Lift the flap and put four drops of glue just below the flap fold. Glue the straight side of the mouth against the fold.
- Use a red crayon or marker to draw a smile along the bottom edge of the head.
- Holding the puppet's mouth open, use the crayon or marker to outline the edge of the lower mouth.

5. To make the nose:

- Use the scissors to round off all the corners of the light-pink square to make a circle.
- Use the red crayon or marker to draw two dots in the center of the pig's nose.
- Put a drop of glue on the back of the nose and place it on the pig's face about halfway between the eyes and upper lip.

6. To make the tongue:

- Use the scissors to round off two corners on one short side of the red rectangle.
- Put a drop of glue on the short straight side of the tongue. Glue the tongue to the center of the mouth.

7. To make the ears:

- Cut the 3-inch purple square diagonally in half.
- Put two drops of glue on one side of each triangle. Glue the ears on the back of the head near the top.
- Fold down the corner of each ear for a realistic effect.

The Tiny Squid

I found a little chest
And opened up the lid.
I looked inside and saw
A teeny, tiny squid.

I thought it had ten legs.
I counted and it did.
When I tried to touch it,
It slid away and hid.

-id Word Family

Ask children to look for words in the poem that contain the letters -id. List them on chart paper. Encourage children to think of other words that belong in the -id word family. Add their words to the list.

Word List

squid   lid   did   slid   hid

Making a Squid Puppet

This unusual squid puppet is a great companion to "The Tiny Squid." Help children glue a copy of the poem to the back of the puppet. Encourage them to take it home to share with their families.

Each child needs:

- one small paper bag
- 6- by 9-inch green rectangle (head)
- two 1½- by 1½-inch white squares (eyeballs)
- two 1- by 1-inch blue squares (eyes)
- 3- by 6-inch red rectangle (mouth)
- ten 1- by 9-inch green rectangles (legs)
- scissors
- glue
- black crayon or marker

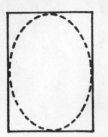

Directions (Review "Puppet-Making Basics," pages 7–9.)

1. To make the head:

- Use the scissors to round off all the corners of the 6- by 9-inch green rectangle to make an oval.
- Glue the head onto the paper bag's flap (bottom) so that the bottom of the oval just covers the flap. The squid's head should extend about three inches beyond the top of the bag.

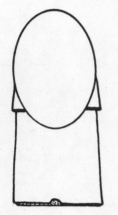

2. To make the eyes:

- Hold both white squares together. Use the scissors to round off all the corners to make circles.
- Repeat with the blue squares.
- Put a drop of glue on each white circle. Press the white eyeballs to the lower part of the head.
- Put a drop of glue on each blue circle and place one at the center of each white eyeball.

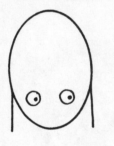

3. To make the mouth:

- Use the scissors to round off two corners on one long side of the red rectangle to make a half circle.
- Lift the flap and put four drops of glue just below the flap fold. Glue the straight side of the mouth against the fold.
- Use a black crayon or marker to draw a smile along the bottom edge of the head.
- Holding the puppet's mouth open, use the crayon or marker to outline the edge of the lower mouth.

4. To make the legs:

- Fold all ten 1- by 9-inch green rectangles accordion-style.
- Put a dot of glue on the front and back of one end of each leg.
- Glue the legs under the mouth and all around.

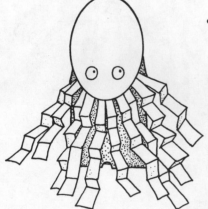

Bear on a Swing

One fine day in spring
A bear sat on a swing.
Then he began to sing.
What a funny thing!

41

-ing Word Family

Ask children to look for words in the poem that contain the letters -ing. List them on chart paper. Encourage children to think of other words that belong in the -ing word family. Add their words to the list.

Word List

swing   spring   sing   thing

Making a Bear Puppet

Use this cuddly bear puppet to introduce the poem "Bear on a Swing." Help children glue a copy of the poem to the back of the puppet. Encourage them to take it home to share with their families.

Each child needs:

- one small paper bag
- 6- by 6-inch brown square (head)
- 6- by 9-inch brown rectangle (body)
- two 4 $\frac{1}{2}$- by 2-inch brown rectangles (arms)
- two 1 $\frac{1}{2}$- by 1 $\frac{1}{2}$-inch white squares (eyeballs)
- two 1- by 1-inch blue squares (eyes)
- 3- by 6-inch red rectangle (mouth)
- 1- by 1-inch black square (nose)
- two 3- by 3-inch brown squares (ears)
- scissors
- glue
- black crayon or marker

Directions (Review "Puppet-Making Basics," pages 7–9.)

1. To make the head and body:
- Use the scissors to round off all the corners of the 6-inch brown square to make a circle.
- Glue the head onto the paper bag's flap (bottom).
- Lift the head and fold back the flap. Put four drops of glue down the center of the paper bag.
- Press the 6- by 9-inch brown rectangle to the bag under the flap.

2. To make the arms:
- Hold both 4½- by 2-inch brown rectangles together. Use the scissors to round off two corners on one short side.
- Put a dot of glue on the front and back of the squared end of each arm piece.
- Glue the arms between the bag and body just below the bear's head and press.

3. To make the eyes:
- Hold both white squares together. Use the scissors to round off all the corners to make circles.
- Repeat with the blue squares.
- Put a drop of glue on each white circle. Press the white eyeballs near the middle of the head.
- Put a drop of glue on each blue circle and place one at the center of each white eyeball.

4. To make the mouth:
- Use the scissors to round off two corners on one long side of the red rectangle to make a half circle.
- Lift the flap and put four drops of glue just below the flap fold. Glue the straight side of the mouth against the fold.
- Use a black crayon or marker to draw a smile along the bottom edge of the head.
- Holding the puppet's mouth open, use the crayon or marker to outline the edge of the lower mouth.

5. To make the nose:
- Use the scissors to round off all the corners of the black square to make a circle.
- Put a drop of glue on the black nose and place it on the bear's face about halfway between the eyes and upper lip.

6. To make the ears:
- Hold both 3-inch brown squares together. Use the scissors to round off all the corners to make circles.
- Glue the circle ears on the back of the head near the top.

Banana Split

I'd love a sweet
Banana split.
I'd share it with
My best friend, Kit.
We'd use our spoons,
We'd sit and sit,
Eating every slurpy bit!

-it Word Family

Ask children to look for words in the poem that contain the letters -it. List them on chart paper. Encourage children to think of other words that belong in the -it word family. Add their words to the list.

Word List

split   it   Kit   sit   bit

Making a Monkey Puppet

Use this cute monkey puppet to bring the poem "Banana Split" to life. Help children glue a copy of the poem to the back of the puppet. Encourage them to take it home to share with their families.

Each child needs:
- one small paper bag
- 6- by 6-inch brown square (head)
- 6- by 9-inch brown rectangle (body)
- two 2- by 3-inch tan rectangles (belly and muzzle)
- two 4 $\frac{1}{2}$- by 2-inch brown rectangles (arms)
- two 1 $\frac{1}{2}$- by 1 $\frac{1}{2}$-inch white squares (eyeballs)
- two 1- by 1-inch blue squares (eyes)
- 3- by 6-inch red rectangle (mouth)
- two 2- by 2-inch brown squares (ears)
- scissors
- glue
- black crayon or marker

Directions (Review "Puppet-Making Basics," pages 7–9.)

1. To make the head and body:
- Use the scissors to round off all the corners of the 6-inch brown square to make a circle.
- Glue the head onto the paper bag's flap (bottom).
- Lift the head and fold back the flap. Put four drops of glue down the center of the paper bag.
- Press the 6- by 9-inch brown rectangle to the bag under the flap.

2. To make the belly:

- Use the scissors to round off all the corners of one tan rectangle to make an oval.
- Glue the tan belly to the center of the monkey's body.

3. To make the arms:

- Hold both 4½- by 2-inch brown rectangles together. Use the scissors to round off two corners on one short side.
- Put a dot of glue on the front and back of the squared end of each arm piece.
- Glue the arms between the bag and body just below the monkey's head and press.

4. To make the eyes:

- Hold both white squares together. Use the scissors to round off all the corners to make circles.
- Repeat with the blue squares.
- Put a drop of glue on each white circle. Press the white eyeballs near the middle of the head.
- Put a drop of glue on each blue circle and place one at the center of each white eyeball.

5. To make the muzzle:

- Use the scissors to round off all the corners of the remaining tan rectangle to make an oval.
- Glue the muzzle to the front of the monkey's face. Align one long edge of the oval to the bottom of the head.
- Use a black crayon or marker to draw two dots for the nose in the center of the muzzle and a smile along the bottom edge.

6. To make the mouth:

- Use the scissors to round off two corners on one long side of the red rectangle to make a half circle.
- Lift the flap and put four drops of glue just below the flap fold. Glue the straight side of the mouth against the fold.
- Holding the puppet's mouth open, use the crayon or marker to outline the edge of the lower mouth.

7. To make the ears:

- Hold both 2-inch brown squares together. Use the scissors to round off two corners on one side.
- Glue an ear to each side of the head. (NOTE: Do not glue the ears on top of the head or the monkey will look like a bear!)

The Snow Family

The cold winds blow.
Here comes the snow.
The snowman says,
"Make my family grow."

The children come
Both fast and slow.
They build four more
All in a row.

-ow Word Family

Ask children to look for words in the poem that contain the letters -ow. List them on chart paper. Encourage children to think of other words that belong in the -ow word family. Add their words to the list.

Word List

snow   blow   grow   slow   row

Making a Snowman Puppet

You don't need snow to create this snowman puppet—a wonderful addition to "The Snow Family." Help children glue a copy of the poem to the back of the puppet. Encourage them to take it home to share with their families.

Each child needs:

- one small paper bag
- 6- by 6-inch white square (head)
- 6- by 9-inch white rectangle (body)
- two 4 $\frac{1}{2}$- by 2-inch white rectangles (arms)
- five 1- by 1-inch black squares (eyes and buttons)
- 3- by 6-inch red rectangle (mouth)
- 1 $\frac{1}{2}$- by 3-inch orange rectangle (nose)
- 4 $\frac{1}{2}$- by 9-inch black rectangle (hat)
- four 1- by 6-inch red, blue, or green rectangles (scarf and hat band)
- scissors
- glue
- black crayon or marker

Directions (Review "Puppet-Making Basics," pages 7–9.)

1. To make the head and body:

- Use the scissors to round off all the corners of the white square to make a circle.
- Glue the head onto the paper bag's flap (bottom).

- Lift the head and fold back the flap. Put four drops of glue down the center of the paper bag.
- Press the 6- by 9-inch white rectangle to the bag under the flap.

2. To make the arms:
- Hold both 4½- by 2-inch white rectangles together. Use the scissors to round off two corners on one short side.
- Put a dot of glue on the front and back of the squared end of each arm piece.
- Glue the arms between the bag and body just below the snowman's head and press.

3. To make the eyes:
- Hold both black squares together. Use the scissors to round off all the corners to make circles.
- Glue the black circles near the middle of the head.

4. To make the mouth:
- Use the scissors to round off two corners on one long side of the red rectangle and make a half circle.
- Lift the flap and put four drops of glue just below the flap fold. Glue the straight side of the mouth against the fold.
- Use a black crayon or marker to draw a smile along the bottom edge of the head and outline the edge of the mouth.

5. To make the nose:
- Cut off one corner of the orange rectangle, as shown. Fold the other end over about half an inch.
- Put a drop of glue on the folded end and place the nose in the center of the snowman's face.

6. To make the hat:
- Fold the black rectangle in half. Holding the folded side, cut off one corner on the open side, as shown, then unfold.
- Take one 1- by 6-inch colored rectangle and glue it on the hat. Trim the band to fit.
- Put three drops of glue on top of the snowman's head. Place the hat on the glue and press.

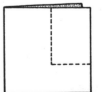

7. To make the scarf:
- Glue one 1- by 6-inch colored rectangle just below the snowman's mouth. Glue the other two rectangles onto the first one at an angle.

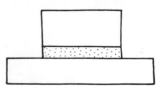

8. To make the buttons:
- Hold the remaining 1-inch black squares together. Use the scissors to round off all the corners to make circles.
- Glue the black buttons to the front of the snowman's body in a line down the middle.

Goat in a Boat

Little goat
In a boat,
How did you get
That bad sore throat?

Little goat
In a boat,
How about wearing
This warm wool coat?

You'll feel better!

-oat Word Family

Ask children to look for words in the poem that contain the letters -oat. List them on chart paper. Encourage children to think of other words that belong in the -oat word family. Add their words to the list.

Word List

goat   boat   throat   coat

Making a Goat Puppet

Invite children to make this goat puppet to go with the poem "Goat in a Boat." Then help them glue a copy of the poem to the back of the puppet. Encourage them to take it home to share with their families.

Each child needs:

- one small paper bag
- 6- by 6-inch gray square (head)
- 6- by 9-inch gray rectangle (body)
- four 4 ½- by 2-inch gray rectangles (arms and ears)
- two 1 ½- by 1 ½-inch white squares (eyeballs)
- two 1- by 1-inch blue squares (eyes)
- 3- by 6-inch red rectangle (mouth)
- 3- by 6-inch gray rectangle (beard)
- 1- by 1-inch black square (nose)
- two 4 ½- by 2-inch yellow rectangles (horns)
- scissors   • glue   • black crayon or marker

Directions (Review "Puppet-Making Basics," pages 7–9.)

1. To make the head and body:

- Use the scissors to round off all the corners of the gray square to make a circle.
- Glue the head onto the paper bag's flap (bottom).
- Lift the head and fold back the flap. Put four drops of glue down the center of the paper bag.
- Press the 6- by 9-inch gray rectangle to the bag under the flap.

2. To make the arms:

- Hold two 4½- by 2-inch gray rectangles together. Use the scissors to round off two corners on one short side.
- Glue the arms between the bag and body and press.

3. To make the eyes:

- Hold both white squares together. Use the scissors to round off all the corners to make circles.
- Repeat with the small squares.
- Put a drop of glue on each white circle. Press the white eyeballs near the middle of the head.
- Put a drop of glue on each blue circle and place one at the center of each white eyeball.

4. To make the mouth:

- Use the scissors to round off two corners on one long side of the red rectangle to make a half circle.
- Lift the flap and put four drops of glue just below the flap fold. Glue the straight side of the mouth against the fold.
- Use a black crayon or marker to draw a smile along the bottom edge of the head and outline the mouth.

5. To make the beard:

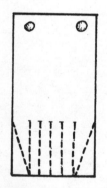

- Cut off two corners of the 3- by 6-inch gray rectangle.
- Make five or six 2-inch cuts on the pointed end. Roll the fringed ends around a crayon to make them curl.
- Put two dots of glue on the squared end of the beard and glue it under the red mouth.

6. To make the nose:

- Use the scissors to round off all the corners of the black square to make a circle.
- Put a drop of glue on the black nose and place it on the goat's face near its upper lip.

7. To make the ears:

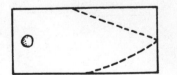

- Hold the remaining two 4½- by 2-inch gray rectangles together. Cut off two corners on one short side.
- Put a drop of glue on the squared end of each ear piece.
- Glue an ear on each side of the goat's head, with the pointed ends facing down.

8. To make the horns:

- Hold both yellow rectangles together. Cut off two corners on one short side (the same as the ears).
- Glue the horns near the top of the head with the pointed ends facing up. Roll the horns around a crayon to make them curl.

Frog on a Log

Once there was a frog
Who sat on a log.
Once there was a dog
Who jumped on that log.
All sank down—
    Frog,
    Dog,
    Log.

-og Word Family

Ask children to look for words in the poem that contain the letters -og. List them on chart paper. Encourage children to think of other words that belong in the -og word family. Add their words to the list.

Word List

frog   log   dog

Making a Frog Puppet

Remembering "Frog on a Log" is easy with this cute frog puppet. Help children glue a copy of the poem to the back of the puppet. Encourage them to take it home to share with their families.

Each child needs:

- one small paper bag
- 6- by 6-inch green square (head)
- 6- by 9-inch green rectangle (body)
- two 4 $\frac{1}{2}$- by 2-inch green rectangles (arms)
- two 2-inch yellow squares (eyeballs)
- two 1 $\frac{1}{2}$-inch blue squares (eyes)
- 3- by 6-inch red rectangle (mouth)
- scissors
- glue
- black crayon or marker

Directions (Review "Puppet-Making Basics," pages 7–9.)

1. To make the head and body:

- Use the scissors to round off all the corners of the green square to make a circle.
- Glue the head onto the paper bag's flap (bottom).
- Lift the head and fold back the flap. Put four drops of glue down the center of the paper bag.
- Press the 6- by 9-inch green rectangle to the bag under the flap.

2. To make the arms:

- Hold both $4\frac{1}{2}$- by 2-inch green rectangles together. Use the scissors to round off two corners on one short side.
- Put a dot of glue on the front and back of the squared end of each arm piece.
- Glue the arms between the bag and body just below the frog's head and press.

3. To make the eyes:

- Hold both yellow squares together. Use the scissors to round off all the corners to make circles.
- Repeat with the blue squares.
- Put a drop of glue on each side of the head. Place the yellow eyeballs on the glue and press.
- Put a drop of glue on each blue circle and place one at the center of each yellow eyeball.

4. To make the mouth:

- Use the scissors to round off two corners on one long side of the red rectangle to make a half circle.
- Lift the flap and put four drops of glue just below the flap fold. Glue the straight side of the mouth against the fold.
- Use a black crayon or marker to draw a smile along the bottom edge of the head.
- Holding the puppet's mouth open, use the crayon or marker to outline the edge of the lower mouth.

5. To make the nose:

- Use the crayon or marker to draw two dots just above the mouth.

Butterfly on My Book

Butterfly, butterfly,
What a flight you took
From the lilac bushes
Over to the brook.

Butterfly, butterfly,
What a flight you took.
You fluttered all around
Then landed on my book.

-ook Word Family

Ask children to look for words in the poem that contain the letters -ook. List them on chart paper. Encourage children to think of other words that belong in the -ook word family. Add their words to the list.

Word List

book   took   brook

Making a Butterfly Puppet

This butterfly puppet serves as a sweet reminder of the poem "Butterfly on My Book." Help children glue a copy of the poem to the back of the puppet. Encourage them to take it home to share with their families.

Each child needs:

- one small paper bag
- 6- by 6-inch green square (head)
- 6- by 9-inch red rectangle (body)
- eight 4 $\frac{1}{2}$- by $\frac{1}{2}$-inch black rectangles (legs and antennae)
- two 1 $\frac{1}{2}$- by 1 $\frac{1}{2}$-inch yellow squares (eyeballs)
- four 1- by 1-inch red squares (eyes and antennae knobs)
- 3- by 6-inch green rectangle (mouth)
- two 6- by 9-inch blue rectangles (wings)
- pieces of colored paper from a scrap box
- scissors
- glue
- black crayon or marker

Directions (Review "Puppet-Making Basics," pages 7–9.)

1. To make the head and body:

- Use the scissors to round off all the corners of the green square to make a circle.
- Glue the head onto the paper bag's flap (bottom).
- Lift the head and fold back the flap. Put four drops of glue down the center of the paper bag.
- Press the red rectangle to the bag under the flap.

2. To make the legs:

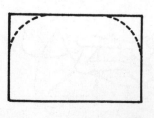

- Fold six 4½- by ½-inch black rectangles accordion-style. Put a dot of glue on the front and back of one end of each leg piece.
- Glue three legs on each side of the body, between the bag and body. Start below the head and work down.

3. To make the eyes:

- Hold both yellow squares together. Use the scissors to round off all the corners to make circles.
- Repeat with two red squares.
- Put a drop of glue on each yellow circle. Press the yellow eyeballs near the middle of the head.
- Put a drop of glue on each red circle and place one at the center of each yellow eyeball.

4. To make the mouth:

- Use the scissors to round off two corners on one long side of the green rectangle to make a half circle.
- Lift the flap and put four drops of glue just below the flap fold. Glue the straight side of the mouth against the fold.
- Use a black crayon or marker to draw a smile along the bottom edge of the head and outline the edge of the mouth.

5. To make the antennae:

- Put a dot of glue on one short end of the two remaining black rectangles. Glue the antennae to the back of the head near the top.
- Hold the remaining red squares together. Use the scissors to round off all the corners to make circles. Glue the circles to the ends of the antennae.

6. To make the wings:

- Hold both blue rectangles together. Use the scissors to round off two corners on one long side.
- Cut off the corners on the opposite side, as shown.
- Decorate the wings by gluing small scraps of colored paper on them.
- Put two drops of glue on the short side of each wing.
- Glue the wings to the back of the bag, behind the legs.

Little Bug

I'm a thirsty little bug
And I've got a little mug.
And when I drink my milk,
I go glug, glug, glug!

I'm a chilly little bug
And I've got a little rug.
In a cozy warm hole
I am snug, snug, snug!

I'm a happy little bug
With my little mug and rug.
The only thing I need
Is a hug, hug, hug!

-ug Word Family

Ask children to look for words in the poem that contain the letters -ug. List them on chart paper. Encourage children to think of other words that belong in the -ug word family. Add their words to the list.

Word List

bug	mug	glug
rug	snug	hug

Making a Bug Puppet

Children will love this adorable bug puppet that goes with the poem "Little Bug." Help them glue a copy of the poem to the back of the puppet. Encourage them to take it home to share with their families.

Each child needs:

- one small paper bag
- 6- by 6-inch purple square (head)
- 6- by 9-inch purple rectangle (body)
- eight 4½- by ½-inch black rectangles (legs and antennae)
- two 1½- by 1½-inch yellow squares (eyeballs)
- two 1- by 1-inch black squares (eyes)
- 3- by 6-inch yellow rectangle (mouth)
- two 1- by 1-inch purple squares (antennae knobs)
- scissors
- glue
- black crayon or marker

Directions (Review "Puppet-Making Basics," pages 7–9.)

1. To make the head and body:
- Use the scissors to round off all the corners of the 6-inch purple square to make a circle.
- Glue the head onto the paper bag's flap (bottom).
- Lift the head and fold back the flap. Put four drops of glue down the center of the paper bag.
- Press the purple rectangle to the bag under the flap.

2. To make the legs:
- Fold six $4\frac{1}{2}$- by $\frac{1}{2}$-inch black rectangles accordion-style. Put a dot of glue on the front and back of one end of each leg piece.
- Glue three legs on each side of the body, between the bag and body. Start just below the head and work down.

3. To make the eyes:
- Hold both yellow squares together. Use the scissors to round off all the corners to make circles.
- Repeat with the black squares.
- Put a drop of glue on each yellow circle. Press the yellow eyeballs near the middle of the head.
- Put a drop of glue on each black circle and place one at the center of each yellow eyeball.

4. To make the mouth:
- Use the scissors to round off two corners on one long side of the yellow rectangle to make a half circle.
- Lift the flap and put four drops of glue just below the flap fold. Glue the straight side of the mouth against the fold.
- Use a black crayon or marker to draw a smile along the bottom edge of the head.
- Holding the puppet's mouth open, use the crayon or marker to outline the edge of the lower mouth.

5. To make the nose:
- Use the crayon or marker to draw two dots in the center of the bug's face near its upper lip.

6. To make the antennae:
- Put a dot of glue on one short end of the two remaining black rectangles.
- Glue the antennae to the back of the head near the top.
- Hold two 1-inch purple squares together. Use the scissors to round off all the corners to make circles.
- Glue the circles to the ends of the antennae.

Clean Cub Club

Messy little lion

Hop into the tub.

Fill it up with bubbles.

Scrub and scrub and scrub.

Take a fluffy towel.

Dry your fur now, rub.

Now you are a member

Of the clean cub club!

-ub Word Family

Ask children to look for words in the poem that contain the letters -ub. List them on chart paper. Encourage children to think of other words that belong in the -ub word family. Add their words to the list.

Word List

cub   club   tub   scrub   rub

Making a Lion Cub Puppet

This lion cub puppet brings the poem "Clean Cub Club" to life. Help children glue a copy of the poem to the back of the puppet. Encourage them to take it home to share with their families.

Each child needs:
- one small paper bag
- 8- by 8-inch brown square (upper mane)
- 6- by 6-inch yellow square (head)
- 6- by 9-inch yellow rectangle (body)
- two 4½- by 2-inch yellow rectangles (arms)
- two 1½- by 1½-inch white squares (eyeballs)
- two 1- by 1-inch blue squares (eyes)
- 3- by 6-inch red rectangle (mouth)
- 1- by 1-inch black square (nose)
- two 3- by 3-inch yellow squares (ears)
- 4- by 8-inch brown rectangle (lower mane)
- scissors   • glue   • black crayon or marker

Directions (Review "Puppet-Making Basics," pages 7–9.)

1. To make the upper mane:
- Use the scissors to round off two corners of the brown square.
- Cut fringes on the rounded sides of the mane, as shown. Do not fringe the straight side.
- Put a drop of glue on each of the four corners of the paper bag's flap (bottom). Glue the mane to the flap, aligning the straight side with the bottom edge of the flap.

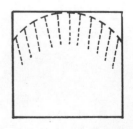

2. To make the head and body:

- Use the scissors to round off all the corners of the 6-inch yellow square to make a circle. Glue the head onto the upper mane.
- Lift the head and fold back the flap. Put four drops of glue down the center of the paper bag.
- Press the 6- by 9-inch yellow rectangle to the bag.

3. To make the arms:

- Hold both $4\frac{1}{2}$- by 2-inch yellow rectangles together. Use the scissors to round off two corners on one short side.
- Glue the arms between the bag and body just below the cub's head and press.

4. To make the eyes:

- Hold both white squares together. Use the scissors to round off all the corners to make circles. Repeat with the blue squares.
- Glue the white eyeballs near the middle of the head. Glue a blue circle to the center of each white eyeball.

5. To make the lower mane:

- Use the scissors to round off two corners on one long side of the brown rectangle.
- Cut fringes only on the rounded side.
- Lift the flap and put four drops of glue below the flap fold. Glue the straight side of the lower mane against the fold.

6. To make the mouth:

- Use the scissors to round off two corners on one long side of the red rectangle and make a half circle.
- Lift the flap and glue the straight side of the mouth against the fold on top of the mane.
- Use a black crayon or marker to draw a smile along the bottom edge of the head and outline the edge of the mouth.

7. To make the nose:

- Use the scissors to round off all the corners of the black square to make a circle.
- Put a drop of glue on the black nose and place it on the cub's face halfway between the eyes and upper lip.

8. To make the ears:

- Hold both small yellow squares together. Use the scissors to round off all the corners to make circles.
- Glue the circle ears on top of the head between the head and the mane.

Home for Beaver, Not Skunk

White teeth, sharp teeth
Chewing on a trunk.
Beaver works all day,
The tree goes KERPLUNK!

White teeth, sharp teeth
Chewing on a trunk.
Building a strong home
For a beaver, not a skunk.

-unk Word Family

Ask children to look for words in the poem that contain the letters -unk. List them on chart paper. Encourage children to think of other words that belong in the -unk word family. Add their words to the list.

Word List

trunk   kerplunk   skunk

Making a Beaver Puppet

This beaver puppet is the perfect companion to "Home for Beaver, Not Skunk." Help children glue a copy of the poem to the back of the puppet. Encourage them to take it home to share with their families.

Each child needs:

- one small paper bag
- 6- by 6-inch brown square (head)
- 6- by 9-inch brown rectangle (body)
- two 4 ½- by 2-inch brown rectangles (arms)
- 3- by 6-inch red rectangle (mouth)
- four 1 ½- by 1 ½-inch white squares (eyeballs and teeth)
- two 1- by 1-inch blue squares (eyes)
- 1- by 1-inch black square (nose)
- two 1 ½- by 1 ½-inch brown squares (ears)
- 4- by 4-inch brown square (tail)
- scissors
- glue
- black crayon or marker

Directions (Review "Puppet-Making Basics," pages 7–9.)

1. To make the head and body:

- Use the scissors to round off all the corners of the 6-inch brown square to make a circle.
- Glue the head onto the paper bag's flap (bottom).
- Lift the head and fold back the flap. Put four drops of glue down the center of the paper bag.
- Press the 6- by 9-inch brown rectangle to the bag under the flap.

2. To make the arms:

- Hold both 4½- by 2-inch brown rectangles together. Use the scissors to round off two corners on one short side.
- Glue the arms between the bag and body below the beaver's head and press.

3. To make the eyes:

- Hold two white squares together. Use the scissors to round off all the corners and make circles.
- Repeat with the blue squares.
- Put a drop of glue on each white circle. Press the white eyeballs near the middle of the head.
- Put a drop of glue on each blue circle and place one at the center of each white eyeball.

4. To make the mouth:

- Use the scissors to round off two corners on one long side of the red rectangle to make a half circle.
- Lift the flap and put four drops of glue just below the flap fold. Glue the straight side of the mouth against the fold.
- Use a black crayon or marker to draw a smile along the bottom edge of the head and outline the edge of the mouth.

5. To make the nose:

- Use the scissors to round off all the corners of the black square to make a circle.
- Put a drop of glue on the black nose and place it on the beaver's face about halfway between the eyes and upper lip.

6. To make the ears:

- Hold both 1½-inch brown squares together. Use the scissors to round off all the corners to make circles.
- Glue the circle ears on the front of the head, near the top.

7. To make the teeth:

- Hold the two remaining white squares together. Use the scissors to round off two corners on one side.
- Glue the teeth to the inside of the upper lip, just below the nose.

8. To make the tail:

- Use the scissors to round off two corners of one side of the 4-inch brown square.
- Cut off the corners of the opposite side of the square.
- Draw crisscrossing lines with the black crayon or marker to create a diamond pattern on the tail.
- Fold the narrow end over about one inch. Put three drops of glue on the folded end. Glue the tail to the back of the bag near the bottom with the diamond design facing up. Make sure to leave room for the poem!

Fun in the Sun

School is over,
It's time for fun.
We play outside,
We skip and run.

We ride our bikes.
We like the sun.
We swim and eat
Hotdogs in a bun.

-un Word Family

Ask children to look for words in the poem that contain the letters -un. List them on chart paper. Encourage children to think of other words that belong in the -un word family. Add their words to the list.

Word List

fun   sun   run   bun

Making a Child Puppet

When making this puppet, offer children a variety of skin-toned paper to reflect the different skin colors in your classroom. They'll love creating this "self-portrait" to go with the poem "Fun in the Sun." Help children glue a copy of the poem to the back of the puppet. Encourage them to take it home to share with their families.

Each child needs:

- one small paper bag
- 6- by 6-inch skin-colored* square (head)
- 6- by 9-inch rectangle, any color (shirt)
- two 3- by 3-inch squares, color should match the shirt (sleeves)
- two 4½- by 2-inch skin-colored* rectangles (arms)
- two 1½- by 1½-inch white squares (eyeballs)
- two 1- by 1-inch squares, brown, blue, green, or gray (eyes)
- 3- by 6-inch red rectangle (mouth)
- two 2- by 2-inch skin-colored* squares (ears)
- scissors
- glue
- red crayon or marker
- different colored crayons, markers, or yarn to reflect children's hair colors

* NOTE: Skin colors should reflect the skin colors of children in your classroom. Each puppet should have the head, arms, and ears cut from the same color.

Directions (Review "Puppet-Making Basics," pages 7–9.)

1. To make the head and shirt:
- Use the scissors to round off all the corners of the 6-inch square to make a circle.
- Glue the head onto the paper bag's flap (bottom).
- Lift the head and fold back the flap. Put four drops of glue down the center of the paper bag.
- Press the 6- by 9-inch rectangle to the bag under the flap.

2. To make the sleeves:
- Put a dot of glue on the front and back of the 3-inch squares.
- Glue the sleeves between the bag and shirt below the head.

3. To make the arms:
- Hold both $4\frac{1}{2}$- by 2-inch rectangles together. Use the scissors to round off two corners on one short side.
- Glue the arms to the back of the sleeves and press.

4. To make the eyes:
- Hold both white squares together. Use the scissors to round off all the corners to make circles.
- Repeat with both 1-inch squares.
- Glue the white eyeballs near the middle of the head. Glue a 1-inch circle to the center of each eyeball.

5. To make the mouth:
- Use the scissors to round off two corners on one long side of the red rectangle to make a half circle.
- Lift the flap and put four drops of glue just below the flap fold. Glue the straight side of the mouth against the fold.
- Use a red crayon or marker to draw a smile along the bottom edge of the head.

6. To make the nose:
- Use the crayon or marker to draw two dots for a nose on the center of the face between the mouth and eyes.

7. To make the ears:
- Hold both 2-inch squares together. Use the scissors to round off two corners on one side.
- Glue the ears to each side of the head.

8. To make the hair:
- Use crayons or markers to draw the hair, or glue yarn on top of the puppet's head.

Notes

_____

_____

_____

_____

_____

_____

_____

_____

_____

_____

_____

_____

Notes

_____

_____

_____

_____

_____

_____

_____

_____

_____

_____

_____

_____